Network Marketing- The Ultimate Tool

Discover and make use of the powerful secrets of the network marketing to grow better and faster with passive income in real-time.

By
Prateek Sinha

Dedicated to

My Mother and Father

Poonam Sinha and Prem Narayan Sinha

LEGAL NOTICE

This book is © Sinha Academy, All Rights Reserved.

The Publisher has strived to be as accurate and complete as possible in the creation of this book, notwithstanding the fact that he does not warrant or represent at any time that the contents within are accurate due to the rapidly changing nature of the Internet.

While all attempts have been made to verify information provided in this publication, the Publisher assumes no responsibility for errors, omissions, or contrary interpretation of the subject matter herein. Any perceived slights of specific persons, peoples, or organizations are unintentional.

Examples of past results may be used occasionally in this work, they are intended to be for purposes of example only. No representation is made or implied that the reader will do as well from using the techniques.

In practical advice books, like anything else in life, there are no guarantees of income made. Readers are cautioned to reply on their own judgment about their individual circumstances to act accordingly.

This book is not intended for use as a source of legal, business, accounting or financial advice. All readers are advised to seek services of competent professionals in legal, business, accounting, and finance field.

Any perceived slight of specific people or organizations, and any resemblance to characters living, dead or otherwise, real or fictitious, is purely unintentional.

About the Author

Prateek Sinha has made his mark on the digital industry, owning an e-book & paperback business among other endeavours. He is the author of more than 50 books in the genres of business and motivation, making money online, affiliate marketing, search engine optimization, social media marketing, entrepreneurship. As well as more than 20 books in the genres of Fiction such as short stories, long tails, Indian Cinematic Heroes , etc.

Apart from being a writer, *Prateek* is also an entrepreneur & the Founder/Director of his own IT Tech firm named HUBNAWAB® ENTERPRISES which was established by him in the year 2017.

Prateek Sinha is a PGDM in Marketing & Finance from Jaipuria Institute of Management, Lucknow, Uttar Pradesh, India. He has a corporate experience of more than 9 Years since he started working officially in the year 2012.

He is also the owner of Sinha Academy which was established in the year 2017 after his tech firm came into operations.

Acknowledgement

First and foremost, I would like to thank God for giving me the courage to write this book. I would like to thank everyone at Sinha Academy for giving me this opportunity to write and publish the book.

Thank you to my mother and my father for always believing in me.

Thanks, to all my HUBNAWAB® ENTERPRISES marketing team members for your support.

Thanks, to my elder brother Prakhar Sinha for inspiring me at all times.

I would like to thank Sinha Academy for giving me the opportunity to write my articles for their official blogs.

Lastly, I would like to thank my critics. Without their criticism, I would never be able to write this book.

- *Prateek Sinha*

Preface

This book peeks into every corner of the network marketing and help you get started with the latest techniques of network marketing which you apply in real-time and gain real results if you want them.

Right from understanding the concept of network marketing to actually making your audience, this book gives you access to the world of unlimited opportunities to explore.

You'll learn for example, how to start network marketing with your target audience in no time.

Chapter 1 focuses on your perception towards network marketing.

Chapter 2 inspects the mindset of the network marketer.

Chapter 3 explains you the profit margins.

Chapter 4 summarizes your down line techniques.

Chapter 5 lets you ease of your burden.

Chapter 6 gives you an idea of consistency.

Chapter 7 focuses on your turnkey system.

Errata

We take immense pride in our work at Sinha Academy and follow best practices to ensure the accuracy of our content to provide with an indulging reading experience to our subscribers. Our readers are our mirrors, and we use their imputs to reflect and improve upon human errors if any, occurred during the publishing processes involved. To let us maintain the quality and help us reach out to any readers who might be having difficulties due to any unforeseen errors, please write to us at :

sinhaacademylko@gmail.com

Your support, suggestions and feedbacks are highly appreciated by the Sinha Academy's Family.

Table of Contents

I. Introduction

II. Chapter 1: A Business Just Like Any Other

III. Chapter 2: The Mindset of a Business Builder

IV. Chapter 3: What is Your Profit Margin?

V. Chapter 4: Down line: An Asset or a Liability?

VI. Chapter 5: Disposing of the Burden

VII. Chapter 6: Consistent Stream of Income

VIII. Chapter 7: Fostering Your Own Turn Key System

IX. Synopsis and Conclusion

Introduction

Dear Network Marketer,

Much thanks to you for setting aside the effort to peruse this book.

This digital book is focused at the overall organization showcasing local area. This book is an absolute necessity read particularly on the off chance that you haven't earn back the original investment in your business. After you finish this book, you will actually want to:

- Understand the ordinary income to building an organization advertising business so you can design your business long haul

- Understand how most of individuals who fall flat in Network Marketing fizzle as a result of absence of income to maintain their business for the time being

- Reduce overheads so you can equal the initial investment quicker

- Reinvest your benefits carefully to control up your business

- Duplicate these standards to your down line and let your organization work for you

"How sure would you say you are that this book will work for my organization?" you inquire? Indeed, the substance here is:

100% Generic yet appropriate to any organization you are in. I understand that most organizations have their own framework, yet the thoughts here are intended to COMPLIMENT and not repudiate your preparation framework just as give you IDEAS TO SUCCEED.

Straight forward and forth right. Individuals who buy digital books typically need data quick and straight forward. I need my per users to have a speedy perused and catch the central matters quick since I realize that you have contributed time understanding this and I realize your time is valuable.

Undertaking Oriented. Simply adhere to the guidelines. I have accomplished practically everything for you so you can save time and exertion.

In the event that every one of my per users can get only one smart thought from the substance of this book, I believe I have achieved my assignment. Don't simply hush up about this data or your down line. Offer them with your up line, sidelines and individuals who are in other organization promoting organizations.

Figure ABUNDANCE and you will be well headed to independence from the rat race!

Here we go...

Note:

On the off chance that you know about the Network Marketing arrangement you would have run over titles like Network Marketing: Survival or Network Marketing: Pitfalls. Obligation Free is composed as an independent book however the exercises gained from those inside the arrangement will help in additional understanding the standards inside this book to control up your business.

Chapter 1: A Business Just Like Any Other

What is the motivation behind beginning a business? To make benefit.

Most organizations go through more cash than they make that is the reason they die.

So for what reason should arrange promoting be any extraordinary?

The basic conviction is that organization showcasing is a business that appreciates in esteem over the long haul. As such, on the off chance that I have a gathering of 100 to 1,000 individuals under me purchasing the item and enrolling more, I'd get more extravagant and more extravagant! However, we as a whole realize that.

It isn't the treasure toward the finish of the rainbow. It's SURVIVING the initial a half year to 2 years!

Usually most organization advertisers in another industry ordinarily go through a 6 months experimentation period, hence, it is vital to guarantee that during those 6 preparing months, you deal with your money astutely so you can learn and bring in cash simultaneously.

Very much like in typical business, the vast majority of them come up short inside their initial 2 years of activity and battle to make benefit regardless of whether they do endure. The way to endurance is CASH FLOW.

All in all, it tends to be summarized in this condition:

Money today, down line tomorrow.

Individuals in network promoting ordinarily run out of income typically following 3 months and they quit in light of the fact that they spend more as they construct. Yet, by earning back the original investment as quick as could really be expected, it gives gigantic mental solidarity to the wholesaler and the person is less inclined to quitter.

To begin with, we should comprehend the mentality which is the main beginning stage in getting by the initial 3 months.

Chapter 2: The Mindset of a Business Builder

(Try not to continue any further in this book until you imbue these into your cerebrum!)

- It sets aside Effort to assemble an effective business. In the event that you bring in ANY cash in the initial not many months (regardless of whether it is only a couple dollars) it is PERFECTLY NORMAL.

- It is MY BUSINESS. Not my up line's business or my down line's business. Everything relies upon ME investing energy to succeed.

- Invest in TOOLS that acquires income (lead generators, viral digital books, nonexclusive data, and so on) Try not to purchase books and tapes only for getting them.

- Don't utilize your own cash if conceivable. Best finance managers utilize others' cash (acquired cash either from family members or monetary establishments) to construct their business. Recall that income is a higher priority than income.

- Don't blow all your cash on promoting that doesn't acquire income too. Direct reaction promoting is quite possibly the best ways.

- A keen financial specialist doesn't spread himself out something over the top. Fabricate the LOCAL market first. Never adventure outstation except if you have a consistent pay. In the event that you can't deal with yourself, how might you remove care of your down line a long way from you?

- Focus on tackling others' issues. Try not to enlist individuals only for selecting them. Attempt to comprehend what issues they are going through first.

- Enjoying the excursion! Individuals who love their work consistently outflank the individuals who do it hesitantly. On the off chance that your possibility sees you doing your business so hesitantly, will they go along with you?

Chapter 3: What is Your Profit Margin?

One of the vital techniques to create more income is identifying with your COMPENSATION PLAN.

Various plans may vary from one organization to another. A few organizations may flaunt their high payout. They will say something like this:

Our organization is the best since we pay out 75% of our bonus to every one of the merchants! It resembles saying for each $100 deal; $75 is repaid to our kin. You won't ever fall flat with this organization!

I encourage you to settle on clever monetary choices and NOT enthusiastic choices in light of the fact that reacting to passionate allure can cause a ton of feelings of grief later on.

I can't cover every one of the mechanics on plans, yet it is smarter to allude to the book arrangement called Show me The Plan! Where I will clarify more top to bottom about promoting plan mechanics. Yet, with the end goal of this subject, I will list down certain standards (showcasing plan identified with) follow.

- Don't take a gander at the complete payout of the organization; take a gander at the initial 2 degrees of payout: How much you get for enrolling somebody, and the amount you get in the event that THEY select somebody. It is no point dreaming the amount you make as a 'Rainbow Diamond Leader' in the event that you can't prevail at the lower levels

- Examine the amount you need to spend to RECRUIT somebody. A few organizations expect you to one or the other compensation for their preparation program first, or expect you to go with them into the instructional meeting (and you need to take care of yourself)

- If you have little income however wish to join an organization that requires an enormous stock speculation yet high overall revenue, ensure those items can be utilized to SPONSOR your down line so you can recover however much money as could be expected

Chapter 4: Down line: An Asset or Liability?

What is the pay you are anticipating from your business? Do you realize that you need to put time and cash in your down lines? Indeed, the facts demonstrate that you bring in cash when your downline goes along with you or makes a deal, however more often than not, to assemble a drawn out business; you need to put vigorously in their schooling.

Organization Marketing is a business of duplication and albeit numerous individuals will address the cost to assemble their organization, you should be extremely specific of whom you invest your energy with. You can't conceivable be everything to everybody and you should choose who are individuals that you are going spots with!

It bodes well since they time you invest with one methods energy where you could either be fostering another or selecting another wholesaler. Moreover, you need to drive out of your home to see them or go with them in preparing and guiding meetings.

Is it true that you are set up to take care of 'this person'?

More often than not numerous individuals quit network advertising isn't on the grounds that they can't enlist, but since they invest an excessive amount of energy with a select reasoning they can change a duck into a falcon. You quack with ducks however take off with birds, everything being equal. So in the event that you invest an excess of energy with a duck that quacks a great deal yet doesn't do whatever else, you must choose the option to abandon him in the event that you need to take off with the birds (or, more than likely you will resemble the 'duck' too).

The central issue to recall is this:

In the event that you are doing 99% of the work in your organization while the rest is doing 1%: START FINDING NEW DOWNLINES, They will go through less of your cash (and save your opportunity to make more).

In the following not many parts, I will show you how by deleting a portion of the uses on Network Marketing, you and all your down lines can set aside time and cash (so your down lines won't stop effectively because of absence of income and your business will endure better in the previous stages).

Chapter 5: Disposing of the Burden

Here is a bit by bit guidance to ways you can handle the consumption above.

Joining charge and auto-transport:

Rather than going out to begin searching for individuals to join your chance, perhaps the quickest approaches to guarantee income is to LIQUIDATE your items!

See that reserve of items lying around your home? (Your wellbeing supplements, skin health management or water channels, and so on) A many individuals take off from their stocks lying around the house while going on an enlistment binge failing to remember that once you auction every one of your stocks, you will earn back the original investment on your speculation!

On the off chance that you are puzzling over whether to keep those items so you can attempt them yourself, don't stress. There is more where that came from. On the off chance that you strive to dispense with your venture costs, you can generally buy more items from the organization later on and those items will doubtlessly add to your business volume also.

The key is to kick your WARM MARKET off on the items, and not pitch the chance to them straight away! In the event that you attempt a decent item at the grocery store, I am certain you will disclose to them about it. For what reason would it be advisable for you to treat your organization showcasing items any unique? Is it true that you are reluctant to converse with your uncle bounce on the grounds that your items are from an organization showcasing organization?

When you get your loved ones begun the items (It doesn't cost you that much thinking about that those are cash saved for your business whether you sell or part with them), when they get results from it, they will begin elevating the items to individuals around them!

Don't you perceive how by utilizing your stock when you initially got going, you can possibly make runaway verbal giving you free warm leads disconnected? The best thing of everything, you can browse those gatherings of item clients who can be a decent business manufacturer in light of their trust in the item, you can get them in without any problem.

Doing so will likewise dispose of your costs with regards to auto-transport. At the point when individuals are effectively burning-through the item, all your down line will be on auto-boat and you won't fear them dropping their auto-transport since it is taken consideration off by their warm market interest.

Chapter 6: Consistent Stream of Income

A great deal of organization advertisers commit an exceptionally large error in their business. They don't foster various surges of earnings and they depend just on bringing in cash through one source which is the organization they are in. My meaning could be a little clearer.

Suppose I am with XYZ Company. I feel that XYZ Company has the best standing on the planet, the best item, the best advertising plan, has assisted large number of individuals on the planet with the item and opportunity (you get the thought). Since I am so fascinated with my organization, I will not draw in different surges of pay like purchasing or embracing different results of different organizations. Some even venture to learn just inside their own organization showcasing local area as it were.

Allow me to underscore indeed. Organization Marketing is a BUSINESS. You should be open to groundbreaking thoughts and continually learn (even from other organization advertising organizations!).

As a money manager, you should be sufficiently insightful to adjust to circumstances and take the necessary steps (as long as it is moral) to take care of business.

This implies that your reasoning should be sufficiently adaptable to come out with thoughts that achieve the accompanying advances:

- Generate unlimited leads so you will have an enormous name list

- Create reliable Cash Flow to remain alive in Network Marketing

- Recruit downline and train them to execute every one of these means

How would we achieve the accompanying advances?

(1) Adopt the outlook of bounty. Assist others with getting what they need and next time, they will assist you with getting what you need. Go all out to help other people and don't be parsimonious or calculative.

(2) Focus on fostering a client base by adjusting them through the item. Zero in on taking care of their issues with the item. Regardless of whether you need to invest energy to assemble the compatibility with the client, recall that when the client sees fabulous outcomes from your item, they will sell for you energetically. A fulfilled client's tribute is incredible. Rehash deals from the fulfilled client (and individuals around them) will guarantee a predictable income.

(3) BARTER TRADE your organization's item with organizers from OTHER organizations! In the event that I have heaps of stock from my organization (either through buying in mass or from my auto-transport), odds are, there are organizers in different organizations are more than able to exchange with you since they have heaps of stock moreover. With new kinds of stock in your grasp, you can take advantage of different business sectors and construct affinity with them so you can acquaint them with your fundamental chance. (On the off chance that my organization just sells beautifying agents and no enhancements, I can discover an organizer in the enhancement like and trade items to tap the enhancement market.)

(4) Join partner programs online that produce income in the event that you are Internet clever. Discover associate projects that let you take part for an extremely minimal expense or free. Recall the rule that you need to produce income and assist others with taking care of their issues. This sets you in a place to indeed, fabricate compatibility with your expected possibilities and creates you leads. Viral showcasing utilizing digital books or email is a decent method to redirect traffic to your subsidiary projects and they cost practically nothing.

(5) Give away free data on network promoting (there are heaps of free or minimal expense digital books or viral advertising devices around the net) or compose free articles on your items and post them to your companions, partners or families. For instance: If you are in the wellbeing business, compose (or meet a specialist) an article about broad medical problems or wellbeing supplements that will give your potential possibilities mindfulness on their wellbeing and when they are interested they will ask you for more data. You can impart your item to them subsequently.

Chapter 7: Fostering Your Own Turn-Key System

Organization Marketing is a business for yourself yet not without anyone else.

Despite the fact that there no rigid principle or any sorcery recipe that I can propose, in light of the fact that any framework you choose to make will vary from one organization to another, you can foster your own turn-key framework inside your association.

This means this sort of framework is planned considering the group where you and all your downline all FOLLOW THE SAME SYSTEM as an overall blueprint. Everyone needs to head a similar way collectively and a determined spotlight in accomplishing the group objective is critical.

Here are a few rules I can recommend to you:

- Hold neighborhood instructional courses other than the organization's instructional courses on the web or disconnected with all your colleagues

- Educate all the colleagues about legitimate income rules when assembling the business. Give everybody free material to survey.

- Everyone choose how much exertion should be placed in, for instance, a week after week or month to month target volume to accomplish.

- Training meetings on the most proficient method to utilize online frameworks that create leads or utilizing partner sites (if your organization supports one). You may even cooperate to make your own group site.

- Buddy framework to limit prospecting costs (like heading to the gatherings together or prospecting together)

- Brainstorming thoughts on alternate approaches to save costs (for instance: combining a telephone plan as referenced previously)

The central issue to recollect is this:

Everybody should zero in on after a similar framework in your group!

It is pivotal for duplication. Would you be able to envision 100 individuals all going their own way? It smells like a catastrophe waiting to happen.

A definitive objective is to prepare a group of autonomous, cash creating downlines who are MAKING MONEY and aiding their down lines to do likewise.

Since toward the day's end, how acceptable your turn-key framework turns out ponders intensely you through the accomplishment of your down lines.

Synopsis and Conclusion

Allow me to make a synopsis of the relative multitude of standards in this book.

(1)   Cash stream is a higher priority than income

(2)   Cash today implies more leads, more stance, more training and thus: MORE DOWNLINE

(3)   Expenses can be limited. Spend just on what you truly need for your business

(4)   Make sure your down line succeed. At the point when you help them bring in cash, they will help YOU bring in cash!

The excursion to progress might be long and hard, yet consistently recall that it isn't WHEN you finish the organization promoting race, it is the way you arrive by helping other people en route, go along with you toward the end goal. Never finish the organization advertising race alone without your down line.

Best of luck, and see you at the top someday, sometime!

Thankyou!

www.ingramcontent.com/pod-product-compliance
Lightning Source LLC
Chambersburg PA
CBHW070914220526
45466CB00005B/2215